FUN WITH PRINTS and Special Effects

Written by Sue Nicholson and Deri Robins
Artwork by Melanie Grimshaw and Sarah Morley
Photography by Michael Wicks

Copyright © QEB Publishing, Inc. 2010
Published in the United States by
QEB Publishing, Inc.
3 Wrigley, Suite A
Irvine, CA 92618

A CIP record for this book is available from the Library of
Congress.

ISBN 978-1-59566-765-6

Printed in China

Web site information is correct at the time of going to press.
However, the publishers cannot accept liability for any
information or links found on third-party Web sites.

Picture credits
Key: t=top, b=bottom, r=right, l=left, c=center
The Art Archive Dagli Orti/104 t and c, 106 tr and br, 108 cr
and br, 114 tr, 116 tr
Corbis: Caroline Penn 94 tl/ Kevin Fleming 101 tl/
Corbis/Christie's Images Reza Webistan 112 r/ 118br
Getty images: / Bridgeman Art Library 99 cl
Japan National Tourist Organisation/ 110 r;
Travelsite/ Neil Setchfield, 97 c;
Werner Forman/ British Museum 103 tl.

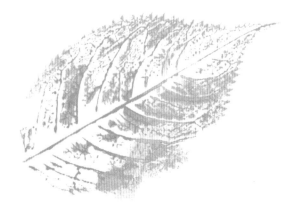

FUN WITH

PRiNTS

and

special

Effects

FUN IDEAS FOR CREATING AMAZING ART!

QEB

QEB Publishing

Contents

WORLD ART

Printing Kit

This section will show you how to make fantastic prints from cardboard, sponges, leaves—even food. You can find almost everything you need from around the home.

Basic equipment
- Paper and cardboard
- Poster/acrylic paints
- Pencils and paintbrushes
- Safety scissors
- White glue
- Ruler

You will also need the extra items listed separately for each project.

Paper and cardboard

You can make prints on white or colored paper, cardstock, posterboard, or cardboard.

Printing blocks

You can make printing blocks from craft foam, sponges, or cardboard.

Paints for printing

The best paints to use are poster paints or acrylic paints. Use fabric paints for printing on cloth.

Don't forget to spread some newspaper to work on, and to wear an apron to keep your clothes clean.

Take care!

Some projects involve cutting, ironing, and photocopying. Always ask an adult for help where you see this sign:

Craft supplies

Keep a big box full of things you can use to make prints. Look out for items with interesting textures or shapes. For example:

- the end of heavyweight corrugated cardboard
- an old sponge or cork
- a piece of yarn
- bubble wrap
- a Lego® brick
- a feather

Brushes and paint dishes

You will need different-size paintbrushes and old dishes for mixing your paints.

A printing roller is also useful for spreading paint evenly on a flat surface.

Materials kit

In this section you will find out to make collages, build three-dimentional models, and create unusual effects using a variety of materials from straws to sequins! Here are some of the things you will need to get started.

Top tip
Don't forget to spread out some newspaper to work on, and wear an apron to keep your clothes clean.

Paper and cardboard
For many of the projects you will need:
• Thin cardboard or thick white paper
• Colored paper
• Tissue paper
• Construction paper
• Thick cardboard from old boxes
But you can use all kinds of paper in your artwork such as newspaper/magazines, shiny card, tracing paper, crêpe paper, brown paper, wallpaper, sandpaper, lacy doilies, used stamps, candy wrappers, kitchen towel or blotting paper, foil, bubble wrap, cereal packets, egg boxes, and kitchen roll tubes, etc.

Safety scissors

Other basics

- Safety scissors
- Sticky tape
- Felt-tip pens
- Pencils and ruler
- Wax crayons
- Poster/acrylic paints and brushes
- White glue

Frame it!

Choose your best work to frame in a simple or decorated card border. Start your own gallery!

Bits and bobs

Keep a box of things with an interesting texture or shape. For example:

- Sequins, buttons, and beads, shells, dried beans, and seeds
- String, yarn, ribbon, and embroidery thread
- Nails, screws, paperclips, and washers

Tools and brushes

Ordinary brushes are useful for backgrounds and details but you might also want some unusual tools. Straws are good for blowing paint and for making paper quills. Toothpicks are good for scraperboard pictures.

Sequins   Glue

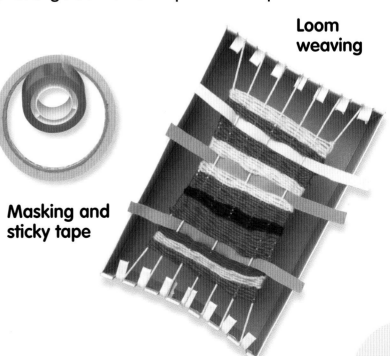

Loom weaving

Masking and sticky tape

Take care!
Some projects involve cutting, gluing, or spraying. Always ask an adult for help when you see this sign:

!

Print Effects

Any pattern made by pressing something down on a surface is printing. You've probably done it by accident! You can make beautiful shapes and textures from ordinary things, and make repeat patterns quickly. Let your imagination go wild!

Basic printing

You have pre-made printing equipment at the end of your fingers! Dip your fingers, thumbs, and the side of your hands into thick paint and press them down onto paper.

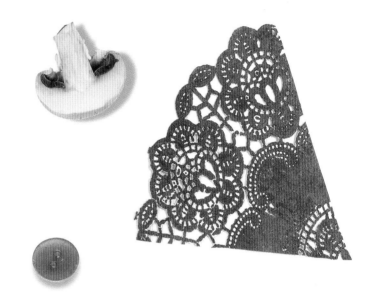

What designs can you make? Use your feet or put on a thick layer of lipstick and press firmly on a piece of paper for luscious lip prints.

Found printers

There are plenty of objects that make wonderful patterns, such as doilies, lace, the ends of straws, tools, keys, and fruit and vegetables.

Broccoli prints

Wheat prints

Feather print

Extra ideas

You could frame your prints, or even wear them! Try making inexpensive giftwrap paper and gift tags that are better than store-bought versions!

Prints can even be used to decorate old furniture, walls, and fabric (but always ask an adult first).

Tip
Try printing on different types of paper: brown paper, newspaper, and tissue all work well. Try using glue instead of paint—sprinkle glitter over while it's wet.

Body Prints

You can make fantastic prints with your hands or fingertips! Just follow these easy steps.

Top tip
Keep a bowl of soapy water and a towel handy. Clean your fingers before you dip them in a new color.

Butterfly frieze

1 Paint green grass and blue sky on a large sheet of paper and leave it to dry.

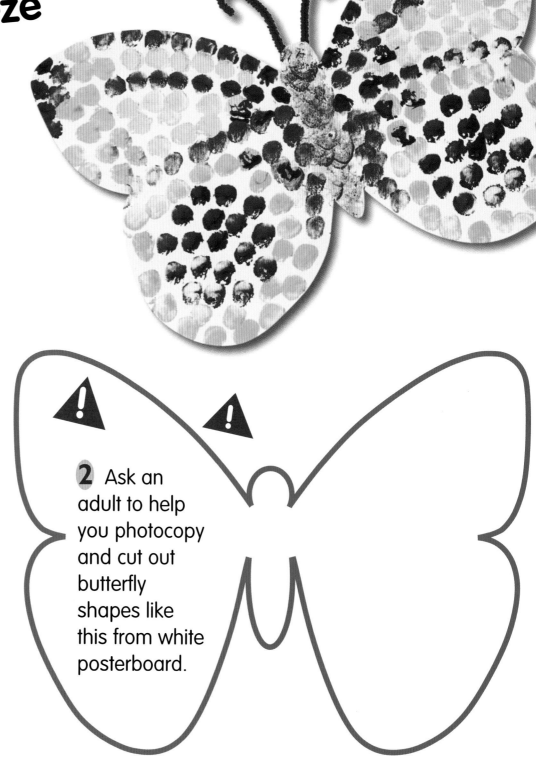

You will need:
- A large sheet of white paper
- Some white posterboard
- Felt-tip pen or pipe cleaners
- Poster paints

2 Ask an adult to help you photocopy and cut out butterfly shapes like this from white posterboard.

Apple prints

1 Paint your palm with red paint and press it onto paper.

2 Make a brown stalk by printing with the side of a short piece of cardboard.

3 Press your thumb into green paint to print some leaves.

3 Dip your fingertips in paint and press them onto the cut-out butterfly shapes.

4 Glue the shapes onto the background. Draw feelers with a felt-tip pen, or glue on pipe cleaners.

Use your fingertips to print these fun animals, then add details with a felt-tip pen.

Click for Art!

To see ancient handprints on cave walls in Australia, go to **www.dvc.vic.gov.au/aav/heritage/mini-posters/14RockArt.pdf**

Leaf Prints

This project shows you how to make
a printed leaf border for a picture or poem.

Top tips
- Make a test print on scratch paper first.
- Leave one color to dry before you add the next.

1 To make the border, draw a straight line 2½ inches (6 centimeters) in from each side of your sheet of construction paper or posterboard. Ask an adult to cut out the middle section for you.

2 Paint the underside of a leaf and press it onto the frame in one corner.

3 Use the same leaf to make prints in the other corners. Coat the leaf with fresh paint each time.

When your border is dry, glue your picture or poem behind it, or use it as a photo frame.

You will need:
- A selection of clean, dry leaves
- Construction paper or posterboard 10 x 12 inches (25 x 30 centimeters)
- Poster paints
- A brush

4 Build up a pattern of leaf shapes in different colors all around the frame. Try beech, sycamore, and oak leaves.

Nature prints

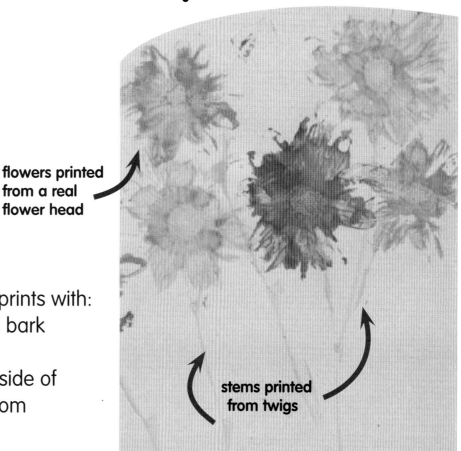

flowers printed from a real flower head

stems printed from twigs

Try making prints with:
- twigs and bark
- flowers
- the underside of a mushroom

Click for Art!

To see leaf designs by William Morris, visit **www.morrissociety.org** Click on the designs and follow the links.

Junk Prints

Pieces of junk, such as nails, screws, cardboard, or thread spools make great prints. But always ask before you use them!

Here are some things to try:
- Corrugated cardboard
- An empty toilet-paper roll
- A scrunched-up paper bag
- Nails, screws, or washers
- An old sponge or cork
- A Lego® brick or puzzle piece

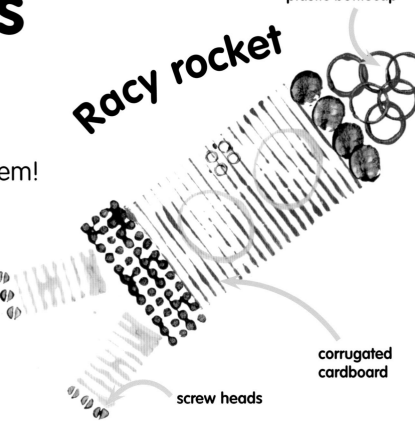

Racy rocket

plastic bottlecap

corrugated cardboard

screw heads

How to make a printing pad

Printing pads use less paint and make a clearer, cleaner print.

Top tip
Don't forget that you will need to make a separate pad for each color.

1 Ask an adult to help you cut a piece of foam to fit in the bottom of a plastic bowl. The easiest way is to place the bowl on top of the foam and draw around it first.

2 Put the foam into the bottom of the bowl and pour over enough paint to cover it. Leave it until the foam soaks up the paint.

Stamping robot

Build up your picture from pieces of junk. Print the junk on scratch paper first to see how it looks.

corrugated cardboard

cork

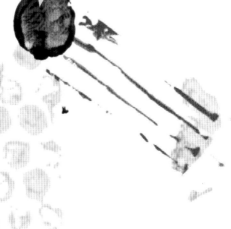

bubble wrap

Lego® brick

3 Press your piece of junk onto the foam, and then press it onto a sheet of paper to make your print.

Food Prints

Print with fruit or vegetables onto fabric to make fun placemats. Ask an adult to help you with cutting and slicing your food.

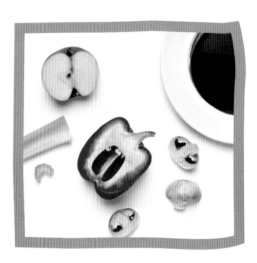

Food shapes and patterns

Look for food with interesting patterns or shapes:
- Dried pasta shapes, such as wheels, long tubes, or butterflies
- A piece of broccoli or cauliflower
- Half an apple or orange
- A large cabbage leaf
- A slice of carrot or celery
- Half a bell pepper

1 Set out the food you are going to print with and some dishes of fabric paint. Sketch your rough design on scratch paper first.

2 Ask an adult to help you cut the fabric for the placemats into rectangles 12 x 10 inches (30 x 25 centimeters). Use pinking shears so the edges don't fray.

Fabric paints
- Be sure to let each color dry before you add an overlapping one.
- Most fabric paints need pressing with a hot iron to stop the colors from washing out. Ask an adult to do this for you.

Click for Art!

To learn all about traditional block printing on fabric in India, go to **www.sashaworld.com/block/block.htm**

Top tip

Wipe the cut surface of fruit or vegetables dry before you paint it. This helps the paint stick better and you will make a clearer print.

3 Dip the food into the paint, or paint the surface of the food with a brush. Press down firmly on the cloth to make the print.

Block Prints

You can make a printing block by gluing a foam shape to cardboard or a small block of wood. Printing blocks can be used over and over again.

You will need:
- Craft foam
- Cardboard, wood, or an empty matchbox for the block
- Poster or acrylic paint
- White glue

1 Draw a simple shape on a piece of craft foam and ask an adult to help you cut it out.

Top tip
If you want to overlap colors, let one color dry before you print the next.

2 Glue the foam shape to a small block of wood, an empty matchbox, or layers of cardboard glued together.

3 With a brush, paint the shape with poster or acrylic paint.

4 Press the shape onto paper to make a repeat pattern.

A simple repeat pattern using one block

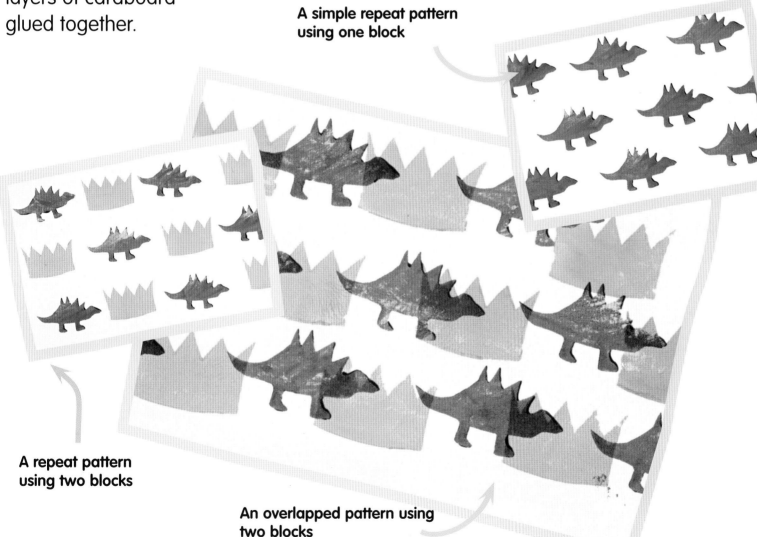

A repeat pattern using two blocks

An overlapped pattern using two blocks

Click for Art!

To see Japanese woodblock prints, go to
www.sfusd.k12.ca.us/schwww/sch618/japan/Art/Art3.html

21

String Prints

Make simple printing blocks by gluing string to small pieces of cardboard or wood. The results are amazing!

You will need:
- Paper or posterboard
- A piece of wood, cardboard, or a piece of styrofoam for the block
- String
- Poster paints
- A brush
- White glue

1 Paint a blue watery background onto paper or posterboard.

2 When the paint is dry, print tall green reeds with the edge of a long piece of cardboard.

Top tip
Sprinkle a little salt onto the blue paint while wet. This will give the background an interesting grainy texture.

3 Glue string to the printing block in a fish shape. Make a large fish block and a smaller one.

4 Glue on string for the fish's scales. Make an eye from string glued in a spiral or a circle of foam.

5 Paint the printing block and press onto the background. Paint the block each time you print.

Simple blocks

You can glue all kinds of things to wood or cardboard to make printing blocks:

- Grains of rice
- Nails, screws, or washers
- Buttons
- A feather
- Paperclips
- An old key

Print fish swimming in the same direction like real fish.

Print reeds behind and on top of the fish, so the fish appear to be swimming through them.

23

Stencil Prints

Cards decorated with stencils are easy to make—and fun to send to your friends!

1 Choose a shape that is symmetrical—the same on both sides.

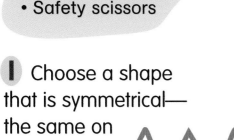

2 Fold a small square of cardboard in half. Draw half the design at the fold.

3 Carefully cut out your stencil and open it out.

4 Fold a sheet of colored cardboard in half lengthwise.

5 Hold your stencil firmly over the front of the card and dab paint through the stencil with a thick, bristly brush.

Top tip
Use a little paint at a time so it does not leak under the stencil.

Giftwrap paper and gift tags

Print stencils in a regular pattern onto plain paper to make a sheet of giftwrap paper.

Print a stencil onto a square of cardboard and hole-punch it to make a matching gift tag.

Click for Art!

To see stencils by Yoshitoshi Mori, go to **www.castlefinearts.com/catalog.aspx?catID=97**

Marbling

In marbling, a beautiful print is made from swirling oil paint dripped into water. Oil and water don't mix, so the oil paint stays on the surface of the water and sticks to the paper when it is gently laid on top.

You will need:

- A large shallow bowl or tray (such as an old plastic bowl or a baking pan)
- Oil paints and mineral spirits
- Pencil, stick, or straw
- Heavyweight white paper

1 Fill your bowl or pan almost to the top with water.

2 With an adult, mix the paint with mineral spirits until the paint is runny. ⚠️

Top tip

When marbling, use just two colors to start with. If you use too many, they will mix together and become muddy.

Marbled collage

Cut shapes of marbled paper and stick them onto a background of different-colored paper so the pictures stand out.

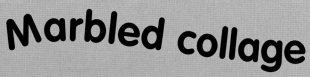

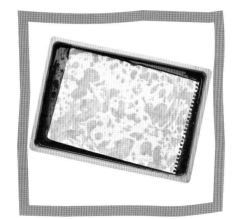

3 Drop tiny blobs of paint onto the water's surface and gently swirl the colors around with a pencil or a stick.

4 Lay your paper on the water's surface. Make sure there are no air bubbles trapped underneath the paper.

Top tip

Instead of stirring the paint with a pencil, try blowing it around the bowl through a straw.

5 Leave for a few seconds, then gently remove the paper. Place the marbled paper on a flat surface to dry.

Click for Art! To see beautiful examples of marbled paper, go to **http://members.aol.com/marbling/marbling**. Click on "28 Examples of marbling."

Mirror Printing

This is one of the simplest and quickest ways to print. The method is always the same, but every print is different.

Easy butterfly print

1 Fold the paper in half. Open it out and paint some thick blobs on one side, roughly in the shape of half a butterfly. Make sure the paint goes right into the fold, but not over it.

2 Fold the paper over. Press down firmly, and then open it up.

Tip
This works well for symmetrical shapes, such as flowers or leaves. See how many designs you can come up with.

Tip
Experiment with string of different thicknesses and texture.

String prints

String prints make fascinating, swirly patterns.

You will need:
- Paper
- Poster paints
- Saucers
- String
- Safety scissors

1 Cut three lengths of string. Put three different-colored poster paints into separate saucers. Put a piece of string in each saucer. Make sure the strings are well coated with paint.

2 Fold a piece of paper in half, then open it back out, as you did for the mirror print. Lay the strings carefully on one side of the paper, with one end of each string sticking out over the edge.

3 Fold the other half of the paper over again and press your hand firmly over the surface. Keeping your hand pressed down, pull out the strings by their ends. Open the paper to see your swirly string picture!

Printing from Card

One of the most common methods of printing is to use blocks. These can be complicated or very simple. You can make your own blocks for printing—the easiest are simple shapes cut out of cardboard.

Print kit

Save as many different types of cardboard as possible—corrugated is great for stripy, textured prints. You can use all parts of the cardboard—the smooth sides are good for printing blocks of color, while the edges are useful for lines and curves. Use the ends of straws or cardboard tubes to make circles or ovals.

Tip

To make your blocks easier to use, glue a small piece of cork or Styrofoam to the back to serve as a handle.

Print a greetings card

Try making blocks for a simple greeting card. You can reuse them to make a batch of cards—perfect for Christmas.

You will need:
- Poster paints • A brush
- Cardboard and paper
- Scissors • Styrofoam

1 Sketch out your ideas for the card design on scrap paper. Keep the shapes simple.

2 Now cut out the shapes you need for your design. You can glue small pieces of Styrofoam to the back to serve as handles.

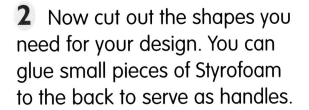

3 Brush the largest printing block with paint. Then press it firmly onto the paper and peel it off to reveal the print beneath.

4 When the first color is dry, do the same with the smaller blocks until your picture is finished. Try not to smudge!

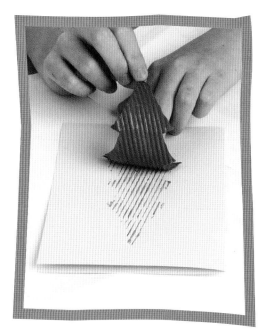

5 You can add details by printing with the top of pen lids.

Tip
Remember when you make a print that the finished print will be a mirror image of your printing block!

Making Blocks

By gluing objects to small pieces of wood, you can make printing blocks that you can reuse over and over again. See what objects you can find around the home, to add to your printing blocks.

Simple kit

Glue string to small pieces of wood or heavyweight cardboard in interesting shapes for simple prints.

Try making shapes from foam, rubber, sponge, old keys, paperclips, dried pasta, buttons, buckles, old toys, or broken jewelry. Almost anything will work!

Let your imagination run wild—but don't forget to ask for permission first.

You can paint on lots of bright colors to get a rainbow effect.

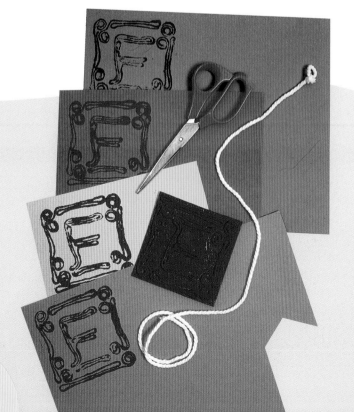

Make a bookplate

Glue string onto one side of a block of wood to form the shape of your initial (remember to do it in reversed mirror writing). Add a few decorations, and use it to print your initial in the front page of your books. You could also use it to make headed notepaper.

Sponge stamps

These are ideal for crisp, clean prints. They are expensive to buy—but you can make your own.

1 Draw a simple design on the soft side of the sponge.

2 Ask an adult to cut away the parts around the design using a craft knife.

3 Brush paint over the raised surface and then press the stamp down onto the paper.

Sponges are also great for smaller patterns, such as wallpaper for a dolls' house. You could even print your own "postage stamps."

Try printing a trail of animal tracks. Glue thin stamps around the outside of a stiff cardboard tube, and use it as a roller printer.

You will need:
• A sponge • A craft knife
• A brush • Poster paint
• Paper

Prints from Nature

Some of the most delicate prints are made from objects from the natural world. Feathers, leaves, flowers, and wood all make intricate prints. Using prints, you can make a pattern that would take hours to paint with a brush.

Print kit

See what natural printers you can find when you are out on a walk. Some, such as feathers and bark, will keep more or less forever, while green leaves will have to be used before they dry out.

Roll or brush poster paint carefully over leaves, ferns, wheatstalks, etc., and press them onto paper to make a print. Experiment with different effects and colors. For example, a white leaf or fern print looks great on dark paper.

Tip
Leaves don't last very long, but you can make longlasting leaf-shaped printers! Just trace around leaves onto heavyweight cardboard, cut them out, and use them as printing blocks.

Leaf prints

Choose three different types of leaf and brush each one with different color of paint to print a pattern.

You will need:
- A collection of leaves— at least three different types
- Bright poster paint
- Paper
- A brush

1 Brush a bright color over one of the leaves, and press it down onto dark-colored paper. Do this several times, then let the paint dry.

2 Take a different leaf, and use a different colored paint. Print onto the paper, overlapping the first leaf prints.

3 Continue printing, until hardly any of the dark background shows through.

Mount your picture on colored paper and place it on your wall.

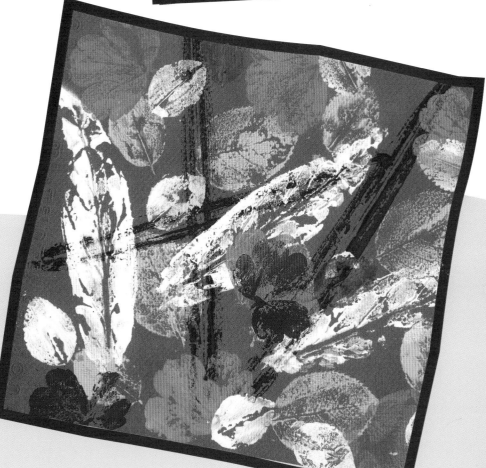

Tip
Try printing while the first color is still wet. Use pastel colors on white paper for an airy, delicate effect.

Potato Prints

A potato print is a cross between printing with food and a block.

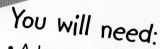

You will need:
- A large potato
- A sharp pencil
- A craft knife
- Poster paints
- Paper
- Brush
- Pencil

Print kit

All you need to make a potato printer is a big potato and a craft knife. Your printer won't last very long, but if you slice off the old design, you can start again on the fresh surface. Other "root" vegetables make good printing blocks, too—try a few and see which ones work best.

1 Ask an adult to cut the potato in half. Draw a simple design on the cut surface with a sharp pencil. Try a butterfly, a flower, or a star.

2 Ask the adult to cut around the design and remove the excess from the edges so your design sticks out. Brush paint over the surface of the design.

3 Press the painted surface firmly onto paper. Rock the printer gently, so that all parts of the design touch the paper.

Try colored paper and contrasting paints for attractive giftwrap.

Your friends and family will much prefer a hand-made gift tag with your own design on it.

Tip

It's fun to make your own gift tags. Cut lots of small rectangles from colored cardboard and fold them in half. Punch a hole in the top-left corner to thread some ribbon through. Then use potato printers to make a design. You could make an interesting border around the edges, too.

Tip

Use a cookie cutter to make an instant printer! Just press the cutter into a potato, and ask an adult to cut away around the outside before removing the cutter.

Tip

Try using different colored paints on different parts of a butterfly to get some really interesting, multi-colored results!

Make a Pop Art Print

The artist Andy Warhol often repeated the same image several times to make bold, bright paintings and prints. Here's how to make a really striking Pop Art print, Warhol-style, for your wall.

You will need:
- A ruler and pencil
- Bright poster paints
- Bubble wrap
- Black felt-tip pen
- A simple printer—this could be a cardboard or wooden block, a potato, or a piece of fruit
- Thick cardboard
- Brushes
- Polyvinyl white glue
- Safety scissors
- Sticky tape
- Yarn

1 Brush brightly colored paint over the bubble wrap, and press it down onto the paper to print a dotty pattern. Do this several times, and use a different color for each piece of paper. Use the ruler and pencil to cut the prints into neat squares, each the same size.

2 Glue the squares to a piece of cardboard to make a checkered effect. Leave a wide border. Brush paint over your printer and press it onto the first square—choose a color that contrasts with the dots. Red and green, blue and orange, and yellow and purple all make good contrasts.

3 Carry on printing onto the squares until every one is filled. Use the black felt-tip pen to go over the lines of each square. Cut some cardboard to make a frame. Paint it in a bright color and then cut a wavy outline with scissors. Tape a loop of yarn to the back so that you can hang it up.

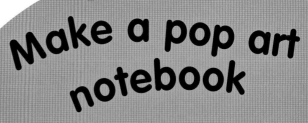

The dots in your picture will make it look like the prints that Andy Warhol made.

Make a pop art notebook

Protect the print with adhesive plastic. Place an open notebook on the back of the print, and draw around it. Draw a border of 2 inches (5 centimeters). Cut flaps in the border, and fold them over the covers of the book, gluing them in place. Glue the first and last pages of the notebook to the covers, to hide the flaps.

Printing Pictures

The more you experiment with different kinds of printers, the more ideas you are likely to get for your pictures. You can mix prints with collage and paint effects, too. Try to think about your prints in a new way—a cabbage leaf print may look just like a cabbage leaf—but it would also make a great tree!

You will need:
- Cabbage leaves
- Thick paints
- Thin, watered-down paints
- Brushes
- Paper
- Thick paper
- White glue
- Safety scissors
- Sticky tape

Trees in the park

In this project, you can use cabbage leaves to create intricate tree shapes that would take a long time to draw or paint.

1 Paint the background very quickly, using a wide, soft brush and thin, watered-down paints. Let it dry (taping it down to your work surface prevents the paper from wrinkling).

2 Now make lots of tree prints, using cabbage leaves of different sizes. Use a good variety of colors, from yellow-green to greens with a brown or bluish shade.

A stippling brush (one with short, stiff bristles) is good for brushing paint onto the cabbage leaf.

3 When the "trees" are dry, cut them out and glue them to the picture. Finish the picture by printing the fence, using the edge of a piece of cardboard brushed with brown paint.

Can you make a print collage like this of your favorite view? Or what about a fantasy landscape—such as a spaceship landing on a distant planet?

Tip
Cauliflower and broccoli make good trees, too. Simple shapes torn from paper make delicate clouds, misty mountains, icebergs, or rough rocks. Sandpaper is perfect for cliffs.

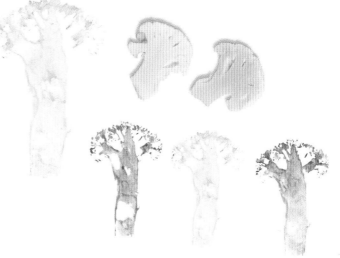

Monoprints

A monoprint is made by pressing a piece of paper over a painted design, and lifting it off. The textures and shapes you get would be impossible to create by painting—they may not always be successful, but when they are, they can be brilliant!

Tip

When you roll your paint out onto the flat surface, try mixing two colors together to create an interesting graduation between one color and the next. Experiment with multicolored monoprints, using lots of different colors.

Print kit

You will need a really smooth surface to print from—a piece of formica, a mirror, or a shiny baking sheet are ideal. Water-based printing inks give the best effects, but you can also use thick paint. Mix the paint with a little dishwashing detergent and white glue to keep it from drying out too quickly. As with the mirror prints on page 28, a monoprint (meaning "one print") can never be repeated.

Take Care !

Be careful if you are using glass to print on—you will need adult help. Check with an adult before you use a table or other piece of furniture to make your monoprint.

Drawing a monoprint

In this project, you draw a shape to create a monoprint beneath.

1 Roll bands of color onto the smooth surface, and place the paper lightly on top.

2 Using a pencil, crayon, or knitting needle, draw a design on the paper—try to press the paper just on the lines you are drawing.

3 Lift up the paper gently, making sure not to smudge the image. Let it dry out completely.

Stencils

Stenciling was very popular among the early pioneers, who couldn't buy wallpaper or decorated furniture. Practice stenciling on paper or cardboard first—when you feel confident enough, you could use the stencils to decorate your bedroom.

Print kit

There are plenty of pre-made stencils to use for printing. You can also buy stencils from craft stores. You will need a brush with short, stubby bristles to make stencils. The paint should be almost dry, and you should dab it over the stencil. This technique is called "stippling."

1 Draw a simple design onto stencil paper or cardboard with a pencil.

2 Ask an adult to cut out the shape with a craft knife.

3 Tape the stencil to the sheet of paper. Using an almost dry brush, stipple the paint over the hole in the stencil, making sure that you go right up to the edges.

Stencil spatter

Instead of stippling your stencil design, you can spatter! Just load the paint onto an old toothbrush, point the brush at the paper, and run cardboard over the bristles. Use interesting shapes such as leaves, keys, or tools. What happens if you move them slightly, and then spatter again with another color?

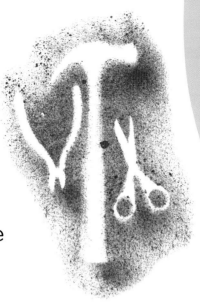

Tip
Use a simple stenciled design to decorate writing paper and matching envelopes. You could also make stencil giftwrap—use spray paint for really quick results.

Spray stenciling

For really quick stenciling, you could use spray paint. Spray paints come in lots of interesting colors, such as silver—as used here.

Tip
You can use your stencils to decorate lots of personal belongings. Ask an adult for help with cutting.

1 Make a large stencil with a repeat pattern. Place it over colored paper and spray paint over it.

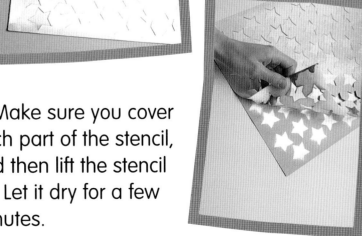

2 Make sure you cover each part of the stencil, and then lift the stencil off. Let it dry for a few minutes.

45

"Me" Collage

Tell a story about yourself through a collage. The theme could be a birthday, a favorite hobby, a vacation—or what about your favorite things? Here are some things you will need:

Top tip
Always ask an adult for help with cutting and gluing.

Soccer collage ideas
A soccer collage could include:
- Team photos
- Scraps from a soccer program
- Ticket stubs from a match
- Newspaper headlines about soccer stars
- Fabric from an old soccer shirt
- Shoelaces or cleats

You will need:
- Materials for your collage
- Cardboard or posterboard
- White glue

1 Collect lots of things that tell a story. If you're not sure what to do, look at the pink and orange boxes on these pages for ideas.

2 Arrange all the things you have collected on a cardboard mount board. Move them around until you are happy with the way they look.

3 Glue down all the things to your piece of mount board with white glue. Glue a small area at a time.

Click for Art!

To see a photocollage by David Hockney, go to **http://artlex.com/** and search for "Photocollage."

Fun collage made from ticket stubs, postcards, and other vacation souvenirs

Vacation collage ideas
- Photographs from travel brochures or magazines
- Ticket stubs and luggage tags
- A sprinkling of sand and shells
- Food and candy wrappers
- Postcards and stamps
- Foreign coins

Magazine Collage

Make a collage from scraps cut or torn from magazines. Choose a theme you find interesting—this one is about food. Look at the collage themes box for other ideas.

Collage themes
- Animals
- Ballet
- Cars
- Colors
- Dinosaurs
- Dogs
- Faces
- Flowers
- Sports
- Happiness
- Horse-riding
- Robots
- Space
- Winter

You will need:
- Plenty of old newspapers and magazines
- Cardboard or posterboard
- Glue

1 Find pictures in magazines about your theme. Using safety scissors, cut out as many pictures as you can.

2 Arrange the pictures on your mount board until you like the way they look.

3 Glue the pictures onto the mount board.

Click for Art!

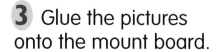

To see collages by Picasso, go to **www.tate.org.uk**, click on "Tate Collection" and find Picasso on the Artists "A-Z."

3D pictures

To make a picture stand out from the cardboard mount:

I Glue the picture onto lightweight cardboard. Cut out around the picture.

2 Fold a strip of cardboard in half, then in half again. Open it out a little, so it looks like a chair with the bottom folded under.

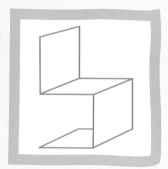

3 Glue the flat part at the top to the mount board.

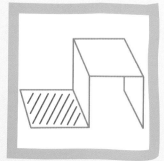

4 Glue the picture to the raised part that sticks out at the front.

Food collage using pictures cut from magazines

49

Paper Collage

You can use all kinds of paper in a collage. Collect plain colored paper, construction paper, giftwrap paper, wallpaper, candy wrappers, tissue paper, and newspaper.

I First plan your picture. Draw the picture lightly with a pencil on the mount board.

Paper parrot

You will need:
- Different colors and textures of paper for the collage
- Mount board
- White glue
- Safety scissors

Top tip
Try using layers of colored tissue papers so the top color mixes with the color below.

This parrot has been made from different kinds of pap cut into shapes, and then glued in place.

Click for Art! To see a collage by Matisse, go to **www.tate.org.uk** click on "Collection," then search "Matisse/The Snail."

2 Using safety scissors, cut out the different kinds of paper into the shapes you want for each part of the picture.

3 Move the pieces of paper around on your drawing until they look right.

4 Glue down the paper shapes, one at a time. To overlap shapes, glue larger pieces first, then smaller ones on top.

Fish shapes cut from foil

Tissue paper strips for seaweed

Sandy ocean floor cut from sandpaper

Collage Face

You don't always have to make collages from simple cardboard! Here are some ideas.

Cardboard crazy!

How many types of cardboard can you find? Try collecting:

- Empty food boxes
- Card stock
- Corrugated cardboard
- Toilet-paper rolls
- Shaped cardboard used for packing
- Lightweight white or colored cardboard

There are lots of ways to make cardboard into different shapes.

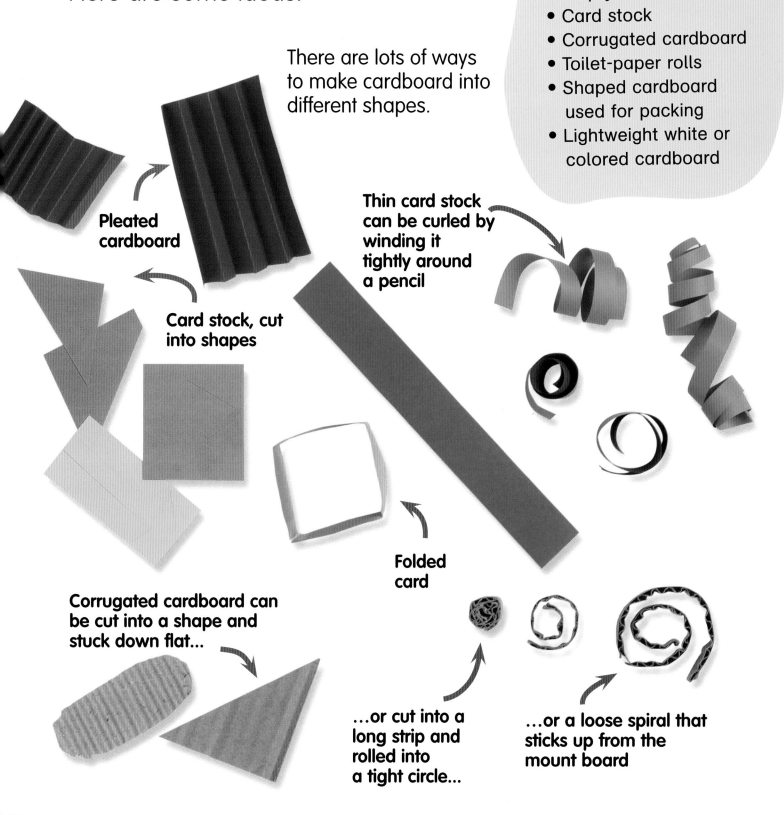

Pleated cardboard

Card stock, cut into shapes

Thin card stock can be curled by winding it tightly around a pencil

Folded card

Corrugated cardboard can be cut into a shape and stuck down flat...

...or cut into a long strip and rolled into a tight circle...

...or a loose spiral that sticks up from the mount board

Life-size body collage

Hair made of thin, green card stock, rolled into spirals

Eyes made out of tightly rolled corrugated cardboard

Ask a friend to lie down on a long piece of paper and draw around him or her with a pencil. Lightly draw in the face. Glue down lots of different materials such as yarn, fabric, felt, torn paper, sequins, or ribbons to make the face and clothes.

Cardboard glued in wavy lines to make the mouth

Earrings made from pleated card stock

Scrap Collage

It's fun to mix different materials and objects in a collage. Here's how to make a picture from scrap materials you may find around your home.

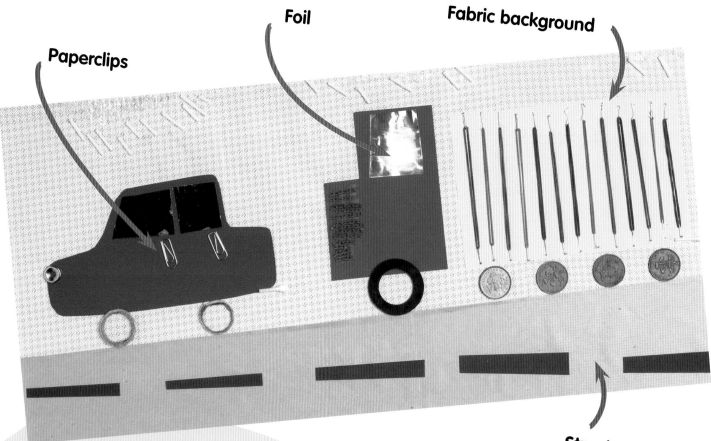

Paperclips

Foil

Fabric background

Street scene made from scrap materials

Collage materials

Look out for these scrap materials to use in your collage:

- Buttons and shells
- String, yarn, and elastic bands
- Scraps of cardboard
- Fabric, ribbon, and thread
- Washers, nuts, bolts, nails, or screws
- Sponges and corks
- Twigs, feathers, and leaves
- Foil and bottle tops
- Bubble wrap, cellophane, and Styrofoam

Junk car

Screws

This car was made from scrap materials glued to corrugated cardboard. It was then spray-painted silver.

Small coins and bottletop wheels

1 Draw the outline of a car on the mount board with a pencil.

2 Using safety scissors, cut shapes out of paper, cardboard, or plastic to fit parts of the car, or arrange items such as buttons, nails, or washers in rows.

3 Keep arranging and rearranging the shapes until you are happy with the way they look.

4 Glue down your collage, one small area at a time.

Click for Art!

To see a collage using scrap plastic and other materials, go to **www.tate.org.uk** click on "Collection" then search on "Tony Cragg" and "Britain Seen from the North."

Food Collage

It's fun to mix different materials and objects in a collage. Here's how to make a picture from leftover dried foods you may find around your home.

1 Glue the black paper onto a strong piece of cardboard as a mount board.

2 Plan your picture on a piece of white paper first. When you are happy with it, draw it onto the black paper with a white or yellow pencil.

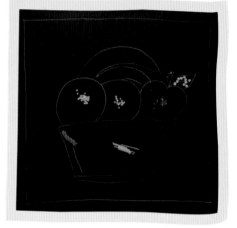

3 Choose dried foods for the different parts of your picture. Sprinkle a few beans, lentils, or seeds in each area to remind you what goes where.

Food collage ideas

Food collages work best if you choose a simple pattern or picture. For example:

★ a flower
★ a tiger
★ a lizard
★ a snake with a zigzag pattern on its back

Top tip

To avoid sticky fingers and messy patches of glue, use tweezers to position items on your collage.

Food collage with border made from pasta wheels

5 Leave the collage flat until the glue has dried completely.

4 Spread glue thickly over a small part of the picture. Sprinkle small seeds over the glue.

Dried foods
- Red and green lentils
- Dried beans and peas
- Pasta shapes and spaghetti
- Black, white, and brown rice
- Sunflower and poppy seeds
- Pine nuts

Fabric Collage

Collages made out of different fabrics are great to look at— and to touch!

Collecting fabrics

Look out for fabrics with different textures, such as scratchy burlap, smooth silk, and soft furs. Buy leftover pieces from stores or junk sales, or cut up old clothes—but always check with an adult first!

You will need:

- Scraps of fabric
- Wide-eye needle and thread (optional)
- Thick cloth or cardboard for the mount
- Safety scissors
- White glue

Working with fabrics

You can use fabrics in a similar way to paper:

- Pleating: Glue the fabric down as you pleat it, or tack it with big rough stitches using a needle and thread.

- Scrunching: Crumple the fabric and glue it down.

- Twisting: Twist the fabric, then glue it in place.

- Braiding: Braid strands of different fabrics into one.

- Cutting: Cut fabric into shapes to stick onto another material, or cut holes so you can see through to the fabric below.

1 Plan your picture and draw it lightly onto the mount.

Click for Art!

To see fabrics used in a collage, go to
www.wetcanvas.com/Articles2/4220/289/page5.php

2 Using safety scissors, cut the fabric into shapes.

3 Arrange the shapes on the mount until you are happy with the way they look. See the pink box for ways of giving your collage an interesting 3D effect.

4 Glue down the shapes, one small area at a time.

Top tip
If you don't want edges of cloth to fray, cut your fabric with pinking shears to give a zigzag edge.

Flowers made from scrunched-up scraps of brightly colored fabric

Clouds made from scraps of netting and lace

Sheep's soft coats made from yarn

Straw Weaving

Woven cloth is good to use in a collage especially if you weave it yourself! To get started, here's how to make a woven wall-hanging using yarn and plastic straws.

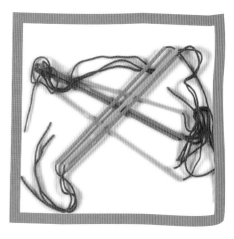

You will need:
- Plastic straws
- Cardboard
- Yarn, string, or embroidery thread for weaving

1 Take some plastic straws and thread a length of yarn through each one. The yarn should be 8 inches (20 centimeters) longer than the straws.

Push this straw down to tighten the threads

Add a second color to make stripes

Top tip
Try wrapping the yarn around a strip of cardboard—this makes it easier to push the threads in and out.

4 Weave a straw at the top and bottom to hold your yarn in place. Your decoration is now ready to hang on the wall.

2 Knot the ends of the yarn loosely together at the top and bottom. Then tape the knots to a sheet of cardboard. Make sure the straws are flat.

3 Weave yarn in and out of the straws from left to right, then right to left. If you like, make some stripes using different-colored yarn.

Making a simple loom

Here's how to set up a simple cardboard loom for the weaving project on page 62.

You will need:
- **A shoebox**
- **Yarn or string for weaving**

1 Ask an adult to help you make a series of notches ½ inch (1.5 centimeters) deep and ½ inch (1.5 centimeters) apart in the sides of a shoebox.

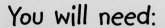

2 Tape the end of a long piece of yarn or string to one side of the box. Wrap the yarn or string around and around the box, using the notches to hold it in place. These are your warp threads.

3 Cut the end of the yarn and tape it to the side of the box.

Now turn to page 62 to get weaving!

Woven Fabric Collage

Use the simple cardboard loom on page 61 to weave fun fabrics for your pictures and collages.

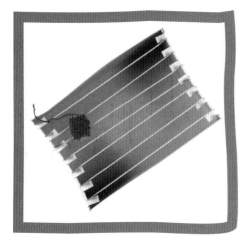

1 Wind a long piece of yarn around a strip of cardboard that you can easily hold in your fingers. Tie the loose end of the yarn around the first warp thread on your loom.

2 Using the card, weave the yarn under and over each of the warp threads to form the weft.

3 At the end of each row, pull the weft threads down toward you, using your fingers.

Top tip

Wind a long thread firmly around each warp thread at the top and bottom of the loom. This gives a neat, strong edge to your woven cloth.

Click for Art!

To see examples of beautiful woven carpets, go to
http://weavingartmuseum.org/main.html

4 Keep weaving until you have covered all the long warp threads. Knot the loose end of the weft thread.

5 Cut the warp threads on the bottom of the box. Knot the threads together. Cut off the extra string or leave it as a fringe.

Fabric collage

Use woven cloth as the background for a fabric collage.

1 Weave strips of fabric and yarn between your warp threads to make bands of different colors and textures.

2 Cut out shapes from felt, such as a moon, star, and a boat.

3 Glue the fabric shapes onto your tapestry with fabric glue, or ask an adult to help you sew them on.

Nature Sculpture

Have fun making outdoor sculptures from smooth stones, fallen flowers and leaves, twigs, moss, or feathers. You can find all the things you need for free in parks, woods, fields, or your own yard!

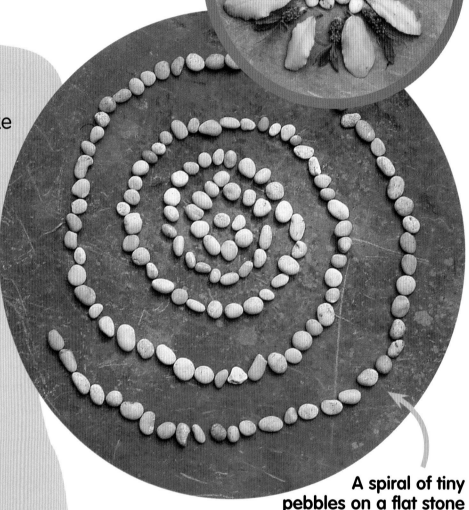

A spiral of tiny pebbles on a flat stone

Sculpture tips

Natural materials can make great outdoor sculptures. Here are some ideas to start you off:

- Arrange berries in a pattern on moss.
- Overlap fallen leaves in the shape of a circle or a star.
- Arrange flower petals on a stone or rock.
- Make rows of pebbles or shells on the beach.
- If it's been snowing, make a sculpture out of snow.
- If it's been raining, trace lines in mud with a sharp stone or twig, then add a pattern of fallen leaves.

Changing nature

Ask a grown-up to photograph your nature sculpture. Go back to it the next day and take another photograph to show how it has been changed by wind, rain, or animals.

Click for Art!

To see nature sculptures by Andy Goldsworthy, go to **www.sculpture.org.uk/image/000000100091**

Colorful petals and leaves on grass

Shells arranged in the shape of a star

65

Glittery Mobile

A mobile is a sculpture that moves. This glittery hanging mobile is fun to watch as it gently twists and spins.

I Ask an adult to help you cut two pieces of dowel, about 12 inches (30 centimeters) long.

You will need:
- Two lengths of dowel rod
- Cellophane or food wrap
- A thick knitting needle
- String or transparent nylon line
- Glitter
- Strip of cardboard
- Glue

Top tip
To add sound to your sparkly mobile, attach tiny bells to the end of some of the glitter curls.

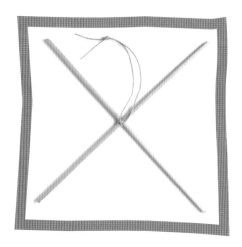

2 Arrange the two pieces of dowel in a cross shape and tie them together at the center with string.

3 Spread out a sheet of cellophane on a flat surface. Tape it down at each corner.

4 Squeeze out some glue, then use a strip of cardboard to shape it into thick blobs with long swirling tails.

5 Sprinkle different-colored glitter on the glue, then let it dry.

6 Carefully peel the glitter curls from the cellophane. Make a small hole in the top of each one with a thick knitting needle.

7 Tie the glitter curls onto the dowel with string or transparent nylon line. Hang up the mobile and watch it twist and twirl!

Click for Art!

To see an interactive virtual mobile, go to **www.nga.gov/kids/zone/zone.htm** and click on "Mobile."

Thumb Pot

This project shows you how to make a simple clay pot and decorate it with lively colors and patterns.

You will need:
- Air-drying clay
- Modeling tools
- Craft glue

Add simple shapes like this star to decorate your pot.

1 Roll the clay into a ball between the palms of your hands. It should be about half the size of a tennis ball.

2 Holding the ball in one hand, push the thumb of your other hand into the middle of the clay.

3 Open out the middle of the pot by gently pinching the sides between your thumb and fingers. Keep turning the pot as you pinch, to keep the sides the same thickness.

4 When you like the pot's shape, flatten the bottom by tapping it gently on a flat surface. Let it dry out a little, then decorate it using modeling tools, or by adding pieces of clay.

Click for Art!

To see examples of clay pottery, go to **www.thebritishmuseum.ac.uk/compass/** and search for "clay pot."

Decorating your pot

Top tip

At step two, don't press down too hard with your thumb or you'll make a hole in the bottom of your pot!

5 When the clay is completely hard, paint your pot with poster paint and let it dry. Finish it off with a coat of craft glue mixed with a little water.

When your clay pot is almost dry, decorate it with a relief pattern or press patterns into the side with modeling tools. If you don't have special pottery tools, use:

- the tip of a pen or pencil
- a large nail
- the end of a ruler
- a blunt metal knife or fork

"Studs" made from flattened balls of clay

Long thin snakes of clay stuck on with a little water

Clay Sculpture

People have been making clay models for thousands of years. For this project, you can use air-drying modeling clay, so you don't need to fire it in a kiln.

1 Tear off a piece of clay and work it into the shape of a head with your fingers.

2 Add features by sticking on extra pieces of clay or cutting away areas. Make hair by squeezing clay through a garlic press so it comes out in strands.

3 Stop when you're happy with how your model looks, and let the clay harden.

Top tip
Coat your finished model with glue mixed with a little water. The glue looks white at first, but dries to a clear, shiny finish.

4 Paint your model with poster paints and let it dry.

Click for Art!

To see sculptures by Henry Moore, go to **www.henry-moore-fdn.co.uk/** Click on the link to "Perry Green," then on the interactive map, then on photos of sculptures.

Animal shapes

Here are some simple animal shapes made out of clay:

71

Junk Robot

You can make fantastic sculptures out of scrap materials! This robot has been made from cardboard boxes and tubes spraypainted silver.

You will need:
- A large cardboard box
- Smaller boxes for the robot's lower body, hands, and feet
- 9–10 toilet-paper tubes
- Corrugated cardboard
- Silver spraypaint

1 Glue down the open top of a cardboard box. Ask an adult to help you make a hole in the top and push in a toilet-paper tube for the robot's neck. Secure it with sticky tape.

2 Glue on a smaller cardboard box to make the lower part of the robot's body. Make two holes underneath and attach toilet-paper tubes for the legs.

3 Tape two toilet paper tubes together to make each of the robot's arms. Secure them to the sides of the robot's body with craft glue.

Click for Art! To see Picasso's "Head of a Bull," a sculpture made with a bicycle seat and handlebars, go to **www.artviews.org/cosby.htm** and scroll down.

Top tip

For a shiny, metallic look, ask an adult to help you spraypaint your robot silver.

4 Cut out ears, eyes, and a mouth from cardboard and glue them to a small cardboard box to make the robot's head.

5 Ask an adult to help you cut a hole in the bottom of the head and attach it to the robot's neck.

6 Glue on feet made from small cardboard boxes. Paint the robot when the glue is dry.

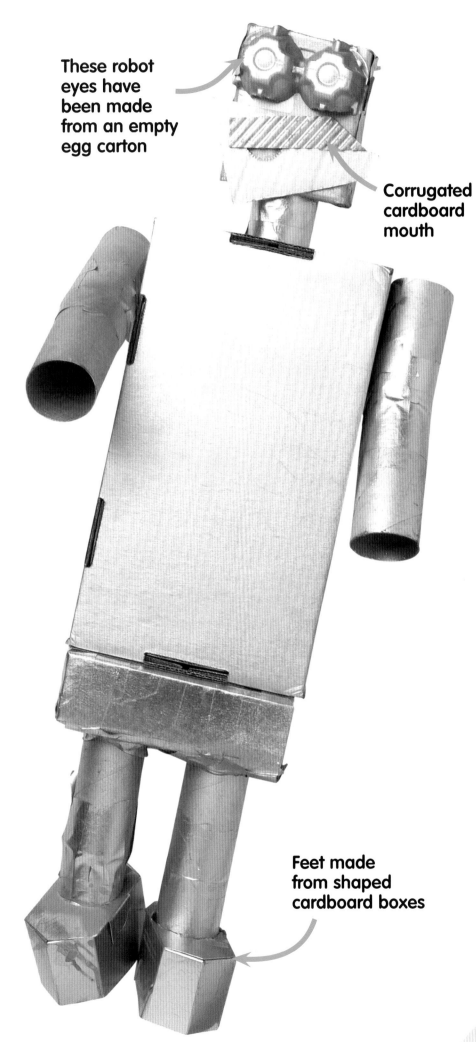

These robot eyes have been made from an empty egg carton

Corrugated cardboard mouth

Feet made from shaped cardboard boxes

Paper Sculpture

This colorful bird has been made out of different kinds of paper that have been folded, creased, or curled to look three-dimensional.

Bird of paradise

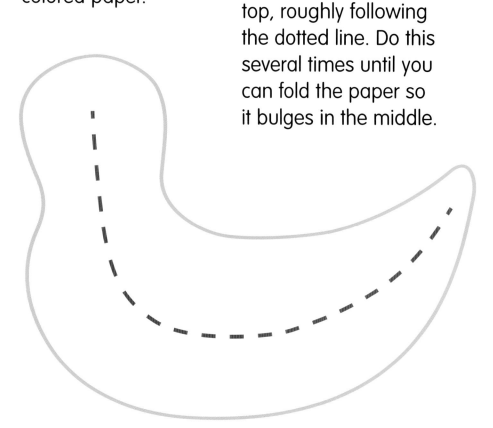

1 Ask an adult to help you copy and enlarge the bird shape below onto two sheets of brightly colored paper.

2 Cut out one of the shapes and crease it with a ballpoint pen top, roughly following the dotted line. Do this several times until you can fold the paper so it bulges in the middle.

3 Do the same with the other shape, but crease it on the opposite side.

4 Ask an adult to help you staple the two pieces of paper together so the sides bulge out. Leave a gap at the bird's head and tail, then stuff it with scrunched-up pieces of newspaper.

74

Plastic "googly eye" bought from a craft store

Paper beak folded and glued in a cone shape

paper decorations

5 Using safety scissors, cut out thin strips of colored paper and wind them tightly around a pen or pencil so they curl.

6 Glue long brightly colored paper curls to make the bird's tail, and shorter curls for the wings.

7 Hang the finished sculpture on the wall with a length of ribbon or yarn.

1 Cut out 6–10 strips of paper about 1 inch (2½ centimeters) wide.

2 Leave two strips 12 inches (30 centimeters) long. Cut two strips 11 inches (28 centimeters) long, and cut two more strips 10 inches (26 centimeters) long.

3 Arrange the strips with the long ones on the outside and the shorter ones in the middle.

4 Staple the strips together at the top and bottom, so the shape balloons out, then hang it up.

Cone Hats

These cute hats are great to make—and fun to wear!

1 Ask an adult to help you draw a big circle on a sheet of cardboard and cut it out with safety scissors. Cut a straight line from the edge of the circle to the exact center.

2 Overlap the edges to make a cone shape that fits your head, then secure the edges together with glue or tape.

3 Paint your hat and decorate it with ribbons, sequins, or glitter.

4 Ask an adult to help you make a hole in each side of the hat. Cut a piece of elastic or ribbon and tie it through the holes.

You will need:

- A large sheet of cardboard
- Ribbons, sequins, stick-on gems, glitter, and feathers for decoration
- A length of elastic or ribbon
- Poster paint, white glue, elastic

Click for Art!

To see sculptural hats designed by Pip Hackett, go to **www.vam.ac.uk/collections/fashion/** and search for "Pip Hackett."

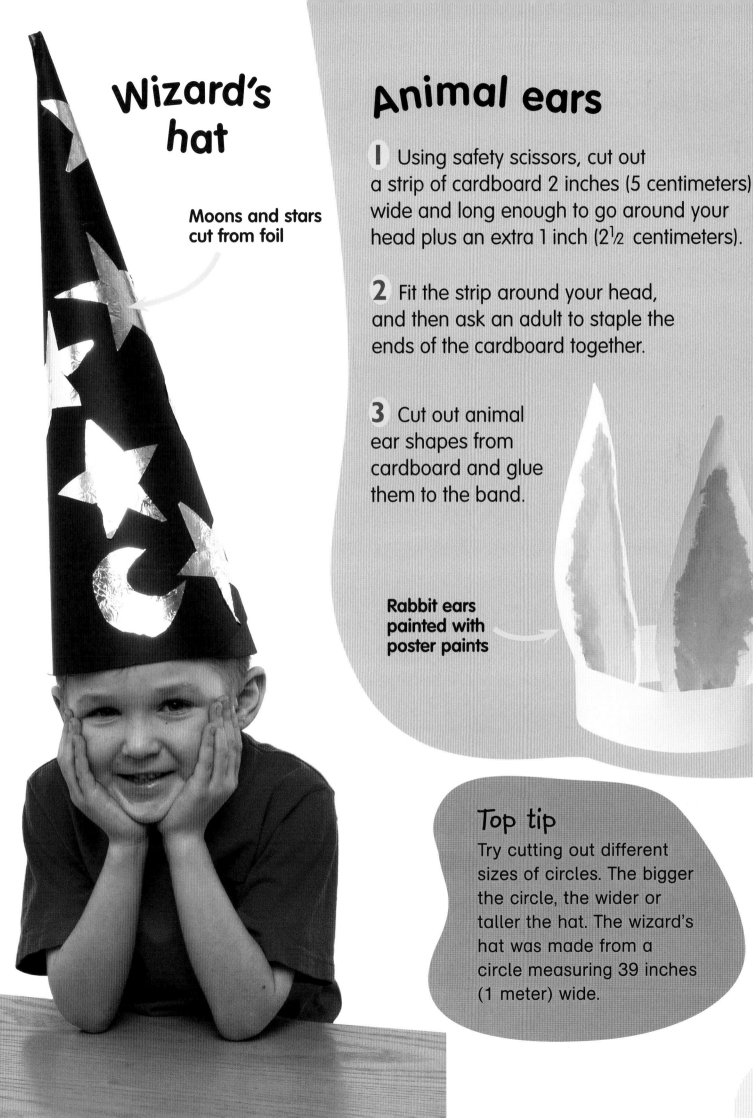

Wizard's hat

Moons and stars cut from foil

Animal ears

1 Using safety scissors, cut out a strip of cardboard 2 inches (5 centimeters) wide and long enough to go around your head plus an extra 1 inch (2½ centimeters).

2 Fit the strip around your head, and then ask an adult to staple the ends of the cardboard together.

3 Cut out animal ear shapes from cardboard and glue them to the band.

Rabbit ears painted with poster paints

Top tip

Try cutting out different sizes of circles. The bigger the circle, the wider or taller the hat. The wizard's hat was made from a circle measuring 39 inches (1 meter) wide.

Ocean Scene

First make and decorate this box for a 3D ocean scene—then turn the page to find out how to fill it with fish and other sea creatures!

1 Cut off the flaps on the open side of the box, or fold them back and glue them to the sides.

You will need:
- A large cardboard box
- Blue cellophane
- Newspaper
- Sandpaper, pebbles, and shells
- Poster paint
- Sticky tape

2 Ask an adult to help you cut a rectangular hole in the top of the box to let in light at the back. Paint the box blue inside and out.

3 Glue a piece of blue cellophane underneath the hole in the top of the box to create a watery blue light.

4 Glue sandpaper, small pebbles, and shells onto the bottom of your box to make a sandy seabed.

Click for Art!

To discover the outdoor sculptures of Oldenburg and van Bruggen: **www.metmuseum.org/explore/oldenburg/artist.html**

5 Scrunch up some old newspaper and pack it tightly into a corner of your box. Secure it in place with tape and glue.

6 Tear more newspaper into strips and glue 2–3 layers over the scrunched-up newspaper, overlapping them as you go.

7 When the glue is dry, paint the newspaper brown or gray, for rocks.

Now turn the page to find out how to make the sea creatures to put in the box.

Ocean Creatures

Now that you've made the box for your 3D ocean scene, it's time to fill it with colorful fish and sea creatures.

You will need:
- Air-drying clay
- A plastic bottle
- Glitter glue
- A clear plastic food bag
- Tissue paper
- Transparent nylon line
- Yarn or string
- White glue

Clay crab and fishes

Use air-drying clay to make these sea creatures for your ocean scene.

Have fun decorating your models with bright colors and spotted patterns!

Plastic bottle fish

These fish were cut out of a large plastic bottle, then painted with wavy and zigzag patterns.

Ask an adult to make a hole at the top of your fish, so you can hang it from the top of your box with transparent nylon line.

plastic bag jellyfish

This sea snail was made from colored air-drying clay

This seahorse was made from cardboard, built up with layers of glued newspaper strips, and then painted

1 Push some colorful scrunched-up tissue paper into a clear plastic food bag.

2 Tie the bag around the middle, then cut the open end into strips for the jellyfish's tentacles.

3 Glue on some big cardboard eyes or some "googly eyes" from a craft store.

Click for Art!

To design a 3D shape on an interactive art site, go to **www.nga.gov/kids/zone/zone.htm** and click on "3D Twirler." You may have to download a program to work it.

Glitter Project

Glitter comes in lots of different colors and can be used to make wonderful, sparkling pictures. Try this rocket idea.

Paint and sparkle

In this project, you use glue-like paint to draw the shapes you want in your picture. Before the glue is dry, add some sparkle!

What you need:
- Colored paper
- Pencil
- Glitter
- White glue
- Brush

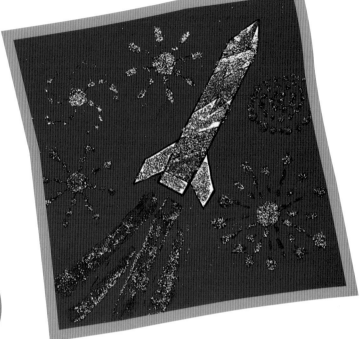

Try making this rocket picture first. Then think of some other pictures that would look good in glitter.

1 Draw the outline of the shapes in your picture in pencil. These are just guides for the glue stage.

2 Use the brush to paint glue into your shapes. You could just use blobs or fill the shapes in.

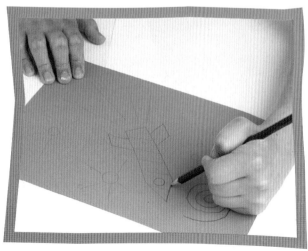

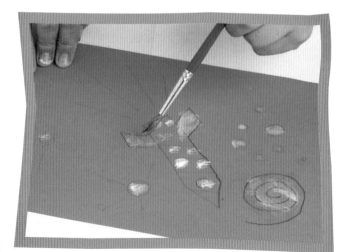

3 Before the glue dries, pick up some glitter and sprinkle it onto the picture. Use different colored glitters for different areas so the finished picture is bright. Leave the glitter on for a few minutes, before blowing off the extra glitter. The rest will have stuck to the glue and made a colorful image.

Tip

You can make your own glitter paint. Just mix some glitter with some glue and use a brush to put the sparkly paint on your paper. Now you can make your own glittering masterpieces.

Material World

You can make fantastic pictures using fabric. Think about different looks and textures when choosing your materials. For example, cotton balls make good fluffy clouds, or you could use lace for a more interesting effect. Have a go at creating your own country scene.

1 First, sketch the outlines of the scene on your paper in soft pencil. It is best to use cardboard because regular paper might tear.

2 Cut out the large background pieces of fabric. You'll need blue for the sky, dark green for hills, and light green for the fields.

3 Now start adding all the details: a fence, a hedge, trees, animals in the fields, clouds, and some flowers.

Tip
Collect old bits of fabric for your pictures. Scraps of white lace are excellent for making clouds or for snowy scenes. Ribbons are handy for creating flowers. Try experimenting with different fabrics for different objects.

Tip
When you have finished your fabric collage, you can paint it with clear varnish. This adds depth and makes the surface of the picture shine. The varnish effect looks great on a dark background.

aper Sewing

Sewing isn't just for fabric. You can also use your needle and thread to make great designs on paper or cardboard. Always ask an adult for help when you want to use a needle. You could even use sewing in one of your paintings!

You will need:
- Posterboard
- Plain paper
- Needle
- Embroidery thread
- Adhesive tape
- White glue

Embroidery house

This simple project will show you the basic method of paper sewing. Try some other designs.

I Draw a simple design on paper. Tape it over the posterboard, and sew thread through the paper and into the board. Discard the paper.

2 On the back of the posterboard, neaten the loose threads. Knot the ends, cut the excess, and put small pieces of tape over the joins.

3 Finally, cut another piece of posterboard slightly larger than the one with the sewing on it. Glue the sewing picture onto this.

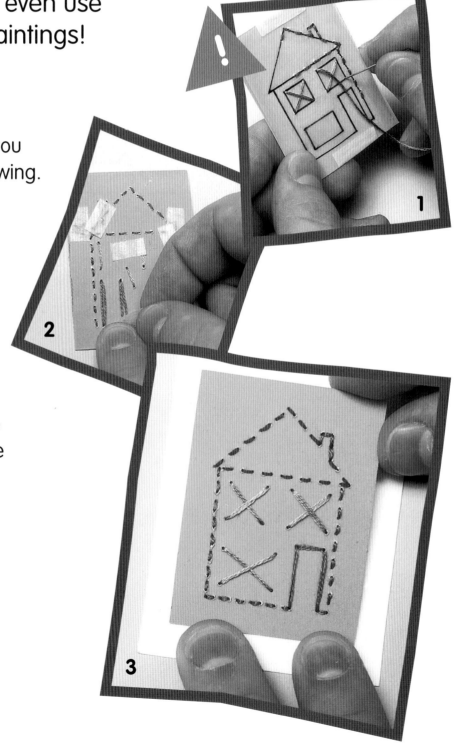

Stitching decorations

There a lots of variations you can use with paper sewing. Try putting colorful beads onto the thread and making zigzag patterns. You can use thread to make decorative borders to your cards and letters—just make sure you use thick enough paper to hold the thread.

Paper pricking

You could also just use the needle to make holes in the paper that show up when light shines through them. This is a technique called paper pricking.

Tip

See if you can use sewing in some of your paintings or collages. You could use thread to make hair, colorful plants in the garden, or even a waterfall. Use different colors of thread together to get interesting results.

As well as decorative borders, you can use sewing to make colorful designs for birthday and Christmas cards. Using the same method as the project on page 85, you can make any shape or design you like.

Creative Collage

Paper and cardboard is cheap, colorful, and easy to cut and paste, which makes it perfect for collage. Keep as many scraps as you can find—you never know when they may come in useful!

You will need:
• Color paper, magazines
• Posterboard or cardboard
• White glue

Making a collage

1 Sketch out a design on cardboard or posterboard.

2 Cut or tear paper shapes to make up the design.

3 Arrange the shapes until you are happy with the way they look and glue them in place.

Mosaic

Try some different techniques in your collages. What about cutting out lots of small, colored squares from old magazines and making them into an image like a Roman mosaic?

Here is another colorful collage made with different types of paper.

Experiment with other materials, too, such as buttons, kitchen foil, and newspaper. You could also paint bits of paper different colors, tear them up, and then use them in your collages. Torn paper creates interesting textures.

You can tear paper into the shapes of animals, flowers, and trees.

Tip

Once you have used paper to make colorful collages, you can go on to make paper sculptures. Cut out the shapes you'll need for your design, then color them before you glue them together. You can make hair by cutting thin strips of paper.

You could even make a sculpture out of paper.

Bits and Pieces

Scraps and remnants from around the home look great in collages: fabric, lace, ribbons, sequins, pasta, beans, and toothpicks. You could probably make a collage from the contents of your wastepaper can!

You will need:

- Fluffy feathers
- String
- Toothpicks
- Colored paper
- Dry leaves
- Beads
- Rice
- White glue
- Cardboard

Perfect pets

1 Draw the outlines of your picture with a pen then cut them out. Cut just inside the lines, so that the pen marks don't show—or turn your cut-out shapes the other way round.

2 Arrange the main shapes on the cardboard. When you are happy with the way they look, glue them down.

3 Now add a bead for the eye, rice flowers, toothpicks and string for the fence, colored paper for the apples, and feathers for the mane and tail.

Still life

All the ingredients in this collage are easy to find. You can adapt it by mixing the collage with painting, and adding other natural materials, such as dried beans, seeds, and pasta.

1 Think how you could make what you've collected into a collage. Sketch the design on a piece of cardboard.

2 Arrange your collection on the pencil outline. Glue it in place.

3 You could leave your collage as it is. Or paint in a background and some flowers among your collage flower heads. Try adding color to some of the objects in the collage if you like.

Using Photos

A camera can be useful in art. You can get all kinds of unusual effects if you combine photos with painting and collage. Keep your eyes open for interesting shots, and save photographs from magazines.

Fantasy fun

1 Want a different home? Take a photo of your house and paint an unusual background to make it look as if you live somewhere different. Look in travel brochures for inspiration.

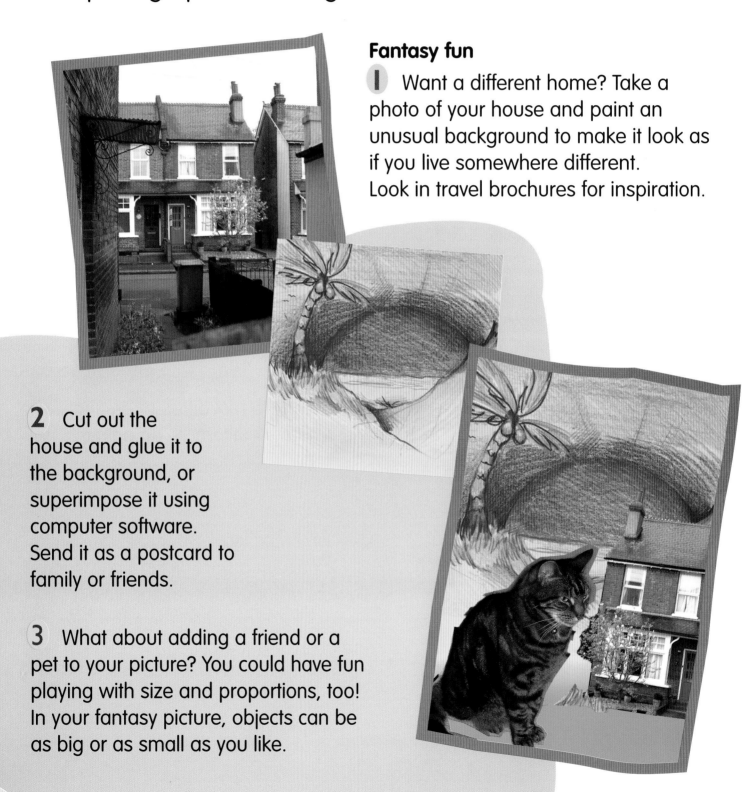

2 Cut out the house and glue it to the background, or superimpose it using computer software. Send it as a postcard to family or friends.

3 What about adding a friend or a pet to your picture? You could have fun playing with size and proportions, too! In your fantasy picture, objects can be as big or as small as you like.

Picture strips

1 Find two photos or magazine pictures, roughly the same size, and divide them into equal sections of ¾ inch (2 centimeters).

2 Cut along the lines to make neat strips.

3 Now glue the first strip from the first picture onto some card, followed by the first strip from the second picture. Keep going, using a strip at a time from each picture, until you've used all the strips.

You can use this effect to mix different animals, or alternate an animal with a photo of a celebrity or a landscape.

Top tip

Try cutting the strips diagonally and horizontally, too.

African Cloth Picture

In Benin, Africa, people tell stories in brightly colored cloth pictures. You can make your own picture using felt.

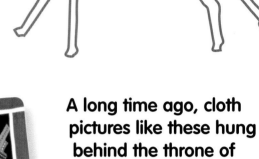

A long time ago, cloth pictures like these hung behind the throne of the king of Benin.

AGADJA 1708-1732
TEGBESSOU 1732-1774
KPENGLA 1774-1789
GUEZO 1818 1858
GLELE 1858-1889
BEHANZIN·1889-1894

You will need:

- Felt (black, red, yellow, orange)
- Felt-tip pen
- Safety scissors

Ask an adult to help you enlarge these animal shapes on a photocopier.

1 Draw an animal with felt-tip pen on the back of a piece of felt. Ask an adult to help you cut it out.

Click for Art!

To see traditional cloth pictures from Benin, visit **www.kidstoafrika.org/benin/tapestries**

Top tip
Cut scraps of different-colored felt and glue them onto your animal shape.

2 Ask an adult to help you cut out a piece of black felt for your background. Make it at least 2 inches (5 centimeters) bigger than your felt shape.

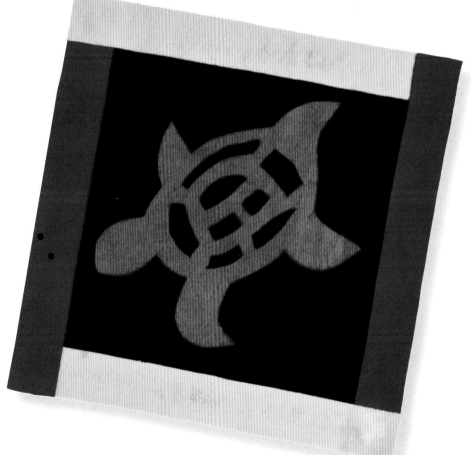

3 Cut out four strips of colored felt 1 inch (2.5 centimeters) wide to make a frame. Overlap the strips at each corner and glue them in place.

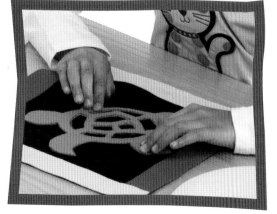

4 Glue your animal picture in the middle of the black background.

Arabian Mosaic

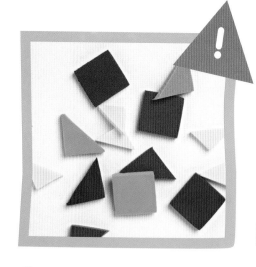

In Islamic countries such as Saudi Arabia, colored tiles are arranged in geometric shapes to make beautiful mosaic patterns.

You will need:
- Craft foam, cut into small squares
- White cardboard
- White glue

1 Ask an adult to help you cut foam squares into triangles, then cut some of the triangles into smaller triangles.

2 Glue a square into the middle of a piece of white cardboard. Glue four small triangles around it.

3 Add four large triangle shapes…

4 …then eight small triangle shapes.

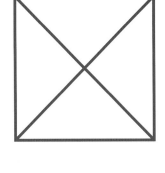

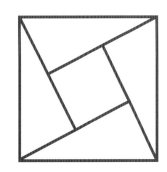
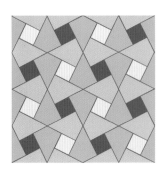

Try copying the shapes on the left to make exciting patterns of your own!

Click for Art!

To see an example of Islamic mosaic art, go to **www.metmuseum.org** and search on "Mihrab."

Islamic tiles with shapes arranged in a geometric pattern.

5 Finish with eight large triangles to form a square.

Celtic Brooch

Make yourself a brooch in the style of the ancient Celts.

1 Draw around the rim of a cup onto cardboard. Ask an adult to help you cut out the circle.

2 Cut out a square of foil, 1½–2 inches (4–5 centimeters) larger than the circle. Place the square over the circle and fold under the edges.

3 Choose a design and carefully trace over it with a soft pencil. Make the lines thick so the design stands out.

4 Place the tracing paper on the foil. Press hard over the lines with a pencil so you make marks in the foil.

98

Top tip
You can also paint your design on the circle with white glue and paint the brooch when the glue is dry. The gold brooch in the picture below has been made like this.

5 Rub black poster paint over the foil, then gently wipe it away with clean cotton balls so black paint is left in the grooves.

6 Tape a safety pin on the back of your brooch with masking tape, so you can wear it. You may like to glue a gemstone in the middle of your brooch.

Jewelry like this beautiful Celtic brooch is still made in Scotland and Ireland.

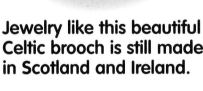

Click for Art!

For examples of Celtic brooches and bracelets, go to **www.thebritishmuseum.ac.uk/compass** and search on "Celtic jewelry."

Chinese Paper Dragon

At New Year, Chinese people dance in the street with huge paper and cloth dragons. Here's how to make a puppet dragon.

1 Trace the dragon's head and tail onto tracing paper, then onto cardboard. Ask an adult to help you cut out the shapes.

2 Paint both sides of a sheet of white paper bright red. When dry, fold the paper in half lengthwise and cut along the fold.

3 Fold the pieces of paper to form an accordion. Glue the two pieces of paper together to make one long piece for the dragon's body.

Ask an adult to enlarge these shapes on a photocopier.

Click for Art!

To learn about dragons in Ancient China go to **www. chinapage.com/dragon1.html**

The dragon dance is performed at Chinese New Year to bring good luck.

plastic "googly" eye

4 Paint the dragon's head and tail bright colors and glue on sequins, glitter, and a "googly" eye.

5 Glue the head and tail to the dragon's body with white craft glue.

6 Glue the chopsticks or popsicle sticks to the head and tail of the dragon.

Indonesian Batik

Traditional batik uses hot wax and dye to make beautifully patterned fabrics. Here's a simple way to make a colorful batik flag.

You will need:
- Plain cotton cloth, such as muslin
- Pinking shears and a dowel stick
- A white wax crayon
- A small paintbrush
- Cold-water dye*, fixative, and salt
- Plastic pail and rubber gloves

1 Ask an adult to help you cut the cloth into a rectangle 10 x 16 inches (25 x 40 centimeters). Use pinking shears so the edge doesn't fray.

2 Draw a picture on one side of the cloth with a soft pencil.

3 Go over your design with the white wax crayon. (The dye will only color the parts that have NOT been covered with wax.)

Click for Art!

To find out about Indonesian batik, go to:
http://members.tripod.com/aberges/

Batik cloth is made in Indonesia, in Southeast Asia.

Using cold-water dye*

Wearing rubber gloves, wet the cloth in clean water. Pour dye into water in an old plastic pail or bowl. Add salt and fixative according to the instructions. Stir well. Put the damp, unfolded cloth into the dye. Leave for one hour, stirring every 5 to 10 minutes. Rinse well in cold water.

*These instructions apply to Dylon® cold-water dye and fixative. For other brands, be sure to follow the manufacturer's instructions.

4 Ask an adult to help you dye the cloth (see the blue box, above).

5 When the cloth is dry, glue a dowel stick down one side on the back to make a flag.

African Mask

Masks are used in all types of African ceremonies. Some represent animals or spirits. They can be made of wood and decorated with shells, beads, fabric, or animal skins. Here's how to make your own African-style mask.

You will need:

- Pear-shaped balloon
- Newspaper
- Wallpaper paste
- Cardboard
- Sticky tape
- White glue
- Poster paints
- Beads, shells, buttons, sequins, raffia, and string
- Pin

African ceremonial masks

1 Blow up a balloon to the size of your head, then knot the end.

2 Follow the instructions on the packet to make some wallpaper paste.

3 Tear newspaper into 1 inch (2½ centimeter) x 2 inch (5 centimeter) strips. Soak them in the paste. Lay the strips neatly across the balloon so they overlap. Add another layer of paper strips and let it dry. Repeat until you have eight layers.

4 When the wallpaper paste is completely dry, pop the balloon with a pin and trim the edges of the paper. Cut out two holes for the eyes.

Tip
Tear, rather than cut, the newspaper. Torn edges lie flatter and overlap more easily.

5 Soak small pieces of paper in water until they break up into little pieces. Mash the paper with a fork, drain off the water, and squeeze until it is almost dry. Mix the pulp with watered-down glue. Use it to build up eyebrows, nose, and mouth.

6 When the glue is dry, paint your mask a wood color. Highlight the features in dark brown, red, and gold paint. Decorate it with shells, beads, or buttons. Add hair made of raffia, yarn, or string.

Egyptian Amulet

The Ancient Egyptians believed that people's spirits must be reunited with their bodies after they died. They decorated dead bodies with amulets, or lucky charms. In this project, you can make a Wedjat-eye charm, which was used by the Egyptians to ward off evil spirits.

You will need:
- Air-drying clay
- Rolling pin or bottle
- Plastic knife
- Wooden or plastic modeling tools
- Poster paint
- Varnish

Ancient Egyptian scarab (beetle) amulets

1 Roll out a piece of clay, until it is ½ to ¾ inch (1–2 centimters) thick and about ¾ inch (2 centimeters) larger than you want your finished eye to be. Carve the outline of an eye on the clay with a modeling tool or pencil. Cut out the shape with a plastic knife.

2 Roll out long, thin pieces of clay and press them into the eye shape to build up the design.

3 Use your tools to make patterns in the clay for decoration.

Tip

Everyday household objects, such as a fork, a blunt nail, or the end of a paintbrush, make great tools.

4 When the model is dry, paint it. Once the paint is dry, add a coat of varnish. Let this first coat dry and then add another.

Tip

To get a smooth surface for decorating, paint an undercoat of white latex paint. Let this dry before adding colored poster paint.

Roman-style Mosaic

Many Roman homes had a mosaic—a picture made of tiny glass, stone, or tile squares called "tesserae"—pressed into the floor. Mosaics showed pictures of many different things.

You will need:
- Graph paper
- Colored paper or white paper and poster paints, or old magazines, or gummed colored paper
- Black construction paper
- Scissors
- White glue

Roman mosaics

1 Plan your design on graph paper, so the finished design is about 9 x 6 inches (22½ x 15 centimeters). Copy this dog mosaic or choose another animal—or your initials. Design a border to frame your design.

Tip

Squares cut from magazines give you different hues of each of your colors, which gives your design more depth.

2 Place the paper with the design on it face-down on the construction paper. Rub the paper with the pencil, so the design transfers onto the sugar paper.

3 Cut equal-size squares from colored paper. Sort each color into a separate pile: blues, greens, reds, etc.

4 Glue the squares onto the construction paper. Leave a gap about ⅛ inch (3 millimeters) wide between each square.

5 To make your mosaic shine, paint it with white glue mixed with water.

Tip

If you want your mosaic to sparkle, cover some squares in glitter glue or paint them in gold or silver metallic paint.

Japanese Banner

In Japan, on Children's Day, children hang up fish-shaped flags on poles outside their homes to bring them good luck. Here's how to make your own fish banner that you can hang up in your room or classroom.

What you need:
- Colored tissue paper
- White glue
- Safety scissors
- Thin cardboard

Japanese fish banners

Tip
When cutting out the scales, fold the paper over so that you can cut lots of scales at once.

1 Cut three shapes out of tissue paper, copying the shapes in the picture above. Choose a different color for each. The fish will fold along the center, so make sure the pieces are big enough.

2 Glue the tail onto one end of the long section, and the head onto the other end.

3 Ask an adult to cut out lots of semicircles of tissue paper for the scales of the fish.

4 Cut out four large circles and two smaller circles to make the eyes. Glue them to the head of the fish.

5 When you have enough scales, add them to the long section of the fish. Glue them from the tail upward, and slightly overlap each row onto the previous one—just like real fish scales.

6 Fold the fish along the center and glue the bottom edges together. Glue a ring of cardboard inside the mouth.

Indonesian Puppets

One of the world's oldest traditions of storytelling, shadow puppets have been popular entertainment in Indonesia for more than 1,000 years. They are called Wayang Kulit. Here's how to make your own Indonesian-style shadow puppet.

You will need:
- Colored construction paper
- Paper
- Cardboard
- Pencil
- Safety scissors and craft knife
- Paper fasteners
- Wooden dowel or wooden skewers
- Adhesive tape
- White sheet
- Electric light

1 Sketch your puppet design roughly on paper. Give it a long nose, long, curling hair, and a curving body and legs.

An Indonesian shadow puppet show

2 When you are happy with your design, draw the figure on cardboard. Draw the arms separately and divide each arm into two parts—shoulder to elbow, and elbow to hand. Round the ends and cut out all the pieces. Ask an adult for help with the craft knife.

3 Tape a stick down the back of one of the puppet's legs, so that the audience cannot see the stick.

5 Tape a thin stick to each of the puppet's hands so you can move its arms.

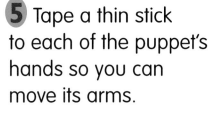

4 Join the arms to the body at the shoulder with paper fasteners. Join the lower and upper parts of the arms at the elbow.

6 To put on a show, suspend a thin white cotton sheet between two chairs. Make sure there are no wrinkles in the sheet. Shine an electric lamp onto the back of the sheet. Kneel down and work the puppet above your head so that your audience see the puppet's shadow. Use one hand to operate one arm, and the other hand to operate the other arm and the head.

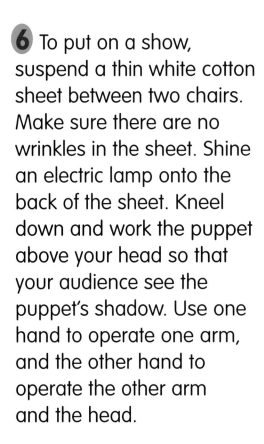

Stained Glass

Stained-glass windows decorated churches and cathedrals in medieval times, and still do today. Make your own window and watch it glow when the light streams through it.

You will need:

- Black construction paper
- White pencil
- Craft knife
- Safety scissors
- Colored tissue paper or colored cellophane
- White glue
- Fine black felt-tip pen

A medieval stained-glass window

1 Plan your picture first. Keep it simple, with bold lines and leave a 1–2-inch (2½ -5 centimeter) border around it for the frame. Now, lightly draw your design on black construction paper with a white pencil. Leave a gap of ¼–½ inch (6–12 millimeters) between the different colors.

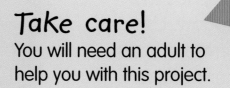

Take care!
You will need an adult to help you with this project.

114

2 Once you are happy with your design, go over the lines again, this time marking them with bold, white outlines.

3 Ask an adult to help you cut out your design with a craft knife. Use a cutting board or several layers of newspaper.

4 Cut tissue paper or cellophane to fit over each window in the paper. Put the pieces in place without glue first to check that they will fit over the holes.

6 Hold the window up to the light. The light will shine through the cellophane, making the colors glow.

5 Glue each piece onto the back of the paper. Put glue around each hole, and try to keep glue off the front of the window.

Tip

As you cut out more construction paper, the frame becomes fragile. Keep a heavy book over the frame so it does not rip while you cut out the remaining pieces.

Moroccan Tile

Take care!
You will need an adult to help you with this project.

In countries such as Morocco, geometric patterns are used to create beautiful tiles.

You will need:

- Thick cardboard, 5$\frac{1}{2}$ inches (14 centimeters) square
- Craft knife
- Masking tape
- Sponge or roller
- Ceramic paint (oil-based or water-based)
- Turpentine (for oil-based ceramic paints. Handle with care!)
- Plain white tile, 6 inches (23 centimeters) square
- Felt

A Moroccan tile

1 Plan out a tile design and practice drawing it. When you are happy with it, draw it onto your cardboard square.

Tip

If you use oil-based paint, ask an adult to clean your brushes in turpentine. A cotton bud dipped in turpentine will wipe away mistakes.

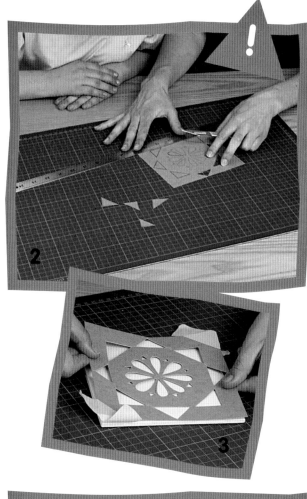

2 Ask an adult to help you cut around the lines with a craft knife. Use a cutting board.

3 Tape the edges of the stencil you have made to a plain, white-ceramic tile.

4 Dab ceramic paint onto the tile through the stencil with a small sponge, brush, or roller. Try to fill all the gaps with paint.

5 Remove the stencil. Let the paint dry if it is oil-based, or ask an adult to help you to fire it in the oven if it is water-based (following the instructions on the pack).

6 Cut out a square of felt. Glue it to the back of your tile so you can put it on a table without scratching it.

Russian Egg

The first Fabergé egg was made in 1885, when the Russian Tsar, Alexander III, commissioned a jeweled Easter egg for his wife from the goldsmith Carl Fabergé. Here's how to "blow" a real egg and decorate it in the style of a fabulous Fabergé egg.

You will need:
- Raw egg
- Pin
- Bowl
- Enamel paints
- Dried lentils, peas, or beans
- Stick-on gems
- White glue
- Brush

1 Use a pin to push small holes through the top and bottom of the egg.

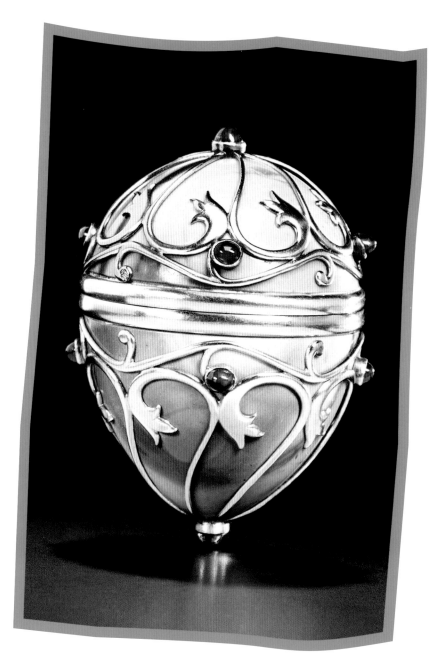

The original Fabergé eggs were made in enamel and decorated with metals, such as silver, gold, and copper, and precious stones.

2 Hold the egg over a bowl and gently blow through one of the holes. The contents of the egg will dribble out until the egg is empty.

3 Holding the egg gently, paint the shell.

4 Decorate the egg using lentils, seeds, sequins, or stick-on gems for jewels. Carefully dot on glue and press one gem, seed, or sequin in place at a time.

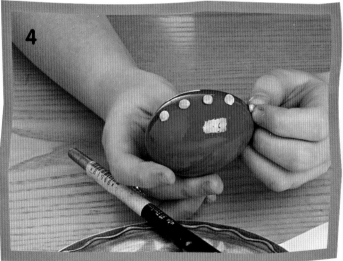

Tip
Use tweezers to pick up tiny seeds or gems, dip them in glue (or paint a layer of white glue on the egg first with a brush), and then drop them into place.

Notes for Parents and Teachers

Creative ideas for prints and special effects in artwork can be inspired from anywhere.

● All art projects should tap into children's interests, and be directly relevant to their lives and experiences. Try using stimulating starting points such as found objects, discussions about their family and pets, hobbies, TV programs, or favorite places.

● Encourage children to source their own ideas and references, from books, magazines, the Internet, or CD-ROM collections.

● Digital cameras can be used both to create reference material (pictures of landscapes, people, or animals) and also used in tandem with children's finished work.

● Give children as many first-hand experiences as possible through visits and contact with creative people.

● Evaluating and talking about art projects will stimulate creativity and appreciation of individuality.

● Help children to judge the originality and value of their creations, to appreciate the different qualities in others' work, and to value ways of working that are different from their own.

Further ideas

● Look at ways of developing the projects further, for example adapting the work into collage, print making, or ceramics.

● Use image-enhancing computer software and digital scanners to enhance, build up, and juxtapose images.